BIBLE STUDIES ON POLITICS

A Study Manual on Key Passages

Richard B. Ramsay

Bible Studies on Politics;
A Study Manual on Key Passages

Richard B. Ramsay

ISBN: 979-8904176983
Staten House

All Scripture quotations are taken from the *English Standard Version,* unless otherwise indicated.

Portions of this booklet are taken from a previous book published by the author, *Intellectual Integrity.*

CONTENTS

PREFACE

Many sincere Christians are confused about important political issues: How should Church and State relate to each other? What is the identity of the People of God now? Is it still the nation of Israel? Does Israel have a God-given right to take back the land it possessed during the Old Testament? What is the purpose of civil government? Should it have authority over religious matters? What does it mean to "render to Caesar the things that are Caesar's, and to God the things that are God's"? How should Christians fulfill our civic duty? Should we try to establish Christianity as the official religion of our country? Should our government enforce Old Testament laws now? What form of government is the best? These are some of the questions we need to answer.

We can't deal thoroughly with these questions in this small booklet, but we can look at some key Bible passages that will give us a good start. Many of these issues are polemical, and we probably won't agree on all of them, but we should be able to find some common ground in the Scriptures.

When I first arrived in Chile as a missionary in 1978, the country was still living under the military regime of Augusto Pinochet (from 1973 until 1990). Naturally, I was curious to hear what the Chileans thought about the situation. But when I began to ask questions, people didn't want to talk about politics, because the topic was too controversial. To this day, Chileans are still extremely sensitive about their views of the political situation at that time.

Politics is even more divisive in other countries. A missionary recently told me that in some churches in the country where he serves, people from different political parties sit on opposite sides of the isle during worship services.

In the United States, where I grew up and where I have lived most of my life, I have observed in recent years that some churches and some denominations are so evidently aligned with a political party that people from another party don't feel comfortable among them. People have left their church because their pastor didn't openly express support for the political cause they embraced.

These are extremes: either keep quiet or argue, either agree or split. It seems like we should be able to talk about politics without fighting or dividing. I want to encourage you to develop a biblical worldview of the subject. Hopefully, we can "renew our minds," bringing our thoughts and our lives more closely in conformity with the biblical teachings.

In this study guide, you first do your own reflection on some passages, answering questions to help you analyze the meaning. Then you will read some comments with suggestions to consider. The comments do not intend to give final answers. You should "test everything" and " hold fast what is good" (1 Thessalonians 5:21). Finally, you will seek practical applications. After the section of Bible Studies, there is a section of additional readings.

My hope is that these Bible studies will be helpful, not just for the United States at this time, but also for many places and for future times. May the Lord guide you, give you wisdom, and encourage you as you study these topics.

The Author

Dr. Ramsay was a missionary in Chile for 21 years, teaching in a seminary and planting churches. There he met his wife, Angelica. They now live in Florida, and they have two adult children. For the past 25 years, they have worked internationally in distance education, traveling to teach classes and producing resources for theological education and leadership training. Richard has taught for *Universidad FLET* and *Thirdmill Seminary* and has developed many online courses.

He holds a D.Min. degree and an M.Div. from *Westminster Theological Seminary*, as well as a Th.M. from *Covenant Theological Seminary.*

Other books by the author include *The Certainty of the Faith, Am I Good Enough?, Basic Greek and Exegesis with Logos and e-Sword, Transformed Into the Image of Jesus, Catholics and Protestants, Strengthen Your Faith, Synopsis of the Bible, Putting the Pieces Together,* and *Orientation for Leaders.*

BIBLE STUDIES

1. Develop a Christian Worldview.

Romans 12:2, John 17:17

For previous reflection

How would you describe your thinking process as you form opinions about current events? How do you usually decide what you think is right or wrong? What are the key things that influence you? Give an example.

◊◊

◊◊

Read the passages.

Romans 12:2
Do not be conformed to this world, but be transformed by the renewal of your mind, that by testing you may discern what is the will of God, what is good and acceptable and perfect.

John 17:17
Sanctify them in the truth; your word is truth.

Analyze the passages.

What do you think "this world" refers to in Romans 12:2?

◊◊

Give an example of what it means to be "conformed to this world."

◊◊

How can we be "transformed" instead of being conformed to this world, according to Romans 12:2? Give an example of what this means.

◊◊

What does this enable us to do?

◊◊

How can we be "sanctified in the truth"? What tool has God given us for this purpose, according to John 17:17?

◊◊

Comments

Christians sometimes suffer from what I call "intellectual schizophrenia." I mean this in the sense of a *divided mind*. When we deal with a subject that we consider theological or "spiritual," we seek answers based on the teachings of the Bible, but when we deal with other topics such as politics, economics, science, or art, for example, our opinions frequently have little to do with our Christian faith. The result is that we develop a fragmented way of thinking.

I remember listening to discussions a few years ago regarding whether the United States should be involved in the war in Iraq. Some were in favor, and others were against it. I don't mean to discuss the issue here; I just want to point out what I observed regarding the way Christians dialogued about it. I heard mostly comments about what might happen if we became involved, or what might happen if we did not become involved. People were predicting what might happen, and making a judgment based almost exclusively on that speculation. I didn't hear much talk about when a war is morally justified. There is a lot of literature on the subject, and there are biblical passages that orient our thinking about war, but these things didn't come up in the conversations. I was just as guilty as anybody else.

But it made me wonder, ¿why do we form our opinions on so many important subjects without reference to the Bible or to our Christian convictions? I had the impression that we were just repeating what we had read somewhere or heard on television. It also seemed that opinions were often based on "consequentialism" rather than biblical principles. That is, we speculate about what might happen, and then make our decision based on what we think would bring the best result.

I remember being shocked when I played basketball with my fellow students at seminary. I couldn't believe the change in personality in some of these future pastors when they walked onto the basketball court! Suddenly they were pushing and shoving and shouting at each other. They called the ball out of bounds when it wasn't really, and they became angry when they lost. I fell into the same pattern.

I see something similar in intellectual matters. Just as we often lack integrity in our actions, we also lack integrity in the way we think. We suddenly change identities when we walk on to the field of politics, economy, art, or science, for example.

We need to develop a "Christian worldview," which I will define as *a mentality formed of biblical principles to think about all areas of life.* We need to learn to think in a Christian way about everything. We could call it a *biblical mindset*. To use an illustration of Calvin, it means putting on Christian "eyeglasses" to see the world.[1]

The Bible gives us the guidelines for studying everything. It adjusts our lenses to see the world more clearly. We might not always find specific Bible passages that deal directly with our topic of study, but biblical principles will always give us a foundation.

---

[1] John Calvin used the illustration of the Bible as eyeglasses to interpret creation in the *Institutes*, Book I, Chapter 6, Paragraph 1.

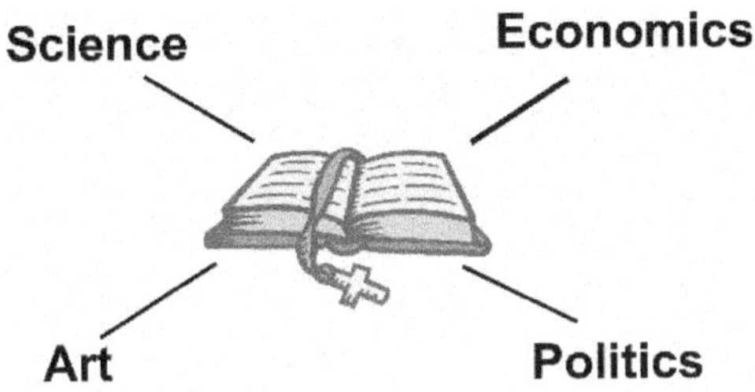

For application

Have you ever formed your opinion about current events based primarily on consequentialism? If so, give an example.

◊◊

Do you sometimes form your opinions about politics based primarily on social media or news? What sources do you use most frequently? Have you investigated the reliability of those sources?

◊◊

In what areas of thought do you think you need to do a better job of developing a biblical worldview, of being "transformed by the renewing your mind"?

◊◊

Mention ways in which you can move in the direction of becoming more consistent with a biblical worldview regarding politics.

◊◊

What other thoughts do you have about the passages studied in this lesson?

◊◊

2. START AT THE BEGINNING.

Genesis 1:26–28

For previous reflection

How do you think the human race would have
developed if sin had not entered the world? Do you
think they would have organized a government and
other institutions? Describe how you imagine it.

◊◊

◊◊

Read the passage.

Genesis 1:26–28
*Then God said, "Let us make man in our image, after
our likeness. And let them have dominion over the fish of
the sea and over the birds of the heavens and over the
livestock and over all the earth and over every creeping
thing that creeps on the earth." So God created man in
his own image, in the image of God he created him; male
and female he created them. And God blessed them. And
God said to them, "Be fruitful and multiply and fill the
earth and subdue it, and have dominion over the fish of*

the sea and over the birds of the heavens and over every living thing that moves on the earth."

Analyze the passage.

What do you think it means that man was made in God's image? What aspects does it include? Think, for example, of the differences between human beings and animals. Think also of the spiritual condition of Adam and Eve before the Fall.

◊◊

◊◊

What did God command Adam and Eve to do? What do you think that would include? Give examples.

◊◊

◊◊

Comments

    Abraham Kuyper, who was a pastor, theologian, and prime minister of Holland, distinguished between an "organic" development and a "mechanical" development of social institutions. On the one hand, the institutions that have developed in an "organic" way are necessary and "natural." They would have developed even without the existence of sin. On the other hand, the institutions

18

that have developed in a "mechanical" way are those that are necessary only because of sin. These are like stakes that a gardener places alongside a small tree so that it will grow straight.[2]

Kuyper argues that even without sin and the results of the Fall, society would have become organized organically, but as one large family in patriarchal form. However, for Kuyper, the State[3] as we know it now, with police, courts, and armies, includes aspects that are only necessary because of sin. In other words, they developed in "mechanical" form.[4]

The distinction between "mechanical" and "organic" development is helpful. We can only speculate about how people would have organized society without sin, but we can assume they would have obeyed the mandate to "be fruitful and multiply," to "fill the earth" and to "subdue it." This is commonly called the "cultural mandate," because it would include the development of all aspects of culture.

Furthermore, the image of God in people would lead them to keep things orderly. As the human race grew, life

---

[2] Abraham Kuyper, *Lectures on Calvinism*, "Calvinism and Politics," and "Politics," talks at Princeton, 1898.< http://www.kuyper.org/main/publish/books_essays/article_17.shtm> , (July 1, 2010).

[3] Terminology can be confusing in the study of politics. Sometimes the term "State" includes the people and territory that are governed, as well as the institution that governs them. Kuyper seems to be using the term that way in this context. The term "civil government" normally refers more specifically the institution that governs the State. Sometimes the two terms are used synonymously. Our main concern in these lessons is the civil government.

[4] See "Abraham Kuyper and Herman Bavinck on Church and State," Jessica Joustra, The Gospel Coalition, Canadian Edition, Feb. 7, 2023. <https://ca.thegospelcoalition.org/article/abraham-kuyper-and-herman-bavinck-on-church-and-state/> (Feb. 21, 2026)

would have become more complicated, requiring more organization and supervision.

To give some examples, they probably would have established guidelines for the exchange of products or the buying and selling of goods. People would have learned to cooperate in the care of their sheep and the cultivation of wheat, possibly in the education of their children. They would have organized many things in a similar way that they have done now after the Fall, but without the damaging effects of sin. *This would be the positive "organic" aspect of the development of society.*

For application

How should the fact that people are made in the image of God influence the way you treat them? How should it affect the way you think about yourself?

◊◊

What does Genesis 1:26–28 tell you about taking care of the earth and our environment? How could you do better at that task? Give examples.

◊◊

What does Genesis 1:26–28 suggest to you about your involvement in politics?

◊◊

3. WHY DO WE NEED A GOVERNMENT?

Romans 13:3-4, 1 Timothy 2:1–2

For previous reflection

How did the entry of sin into the world change the development of human society? How do you think it changed the task of the government? How would you describe the task of the civil government now?

◊◊

◊◊

Do you think the government should be involved in religious matters? Explain your answer.

◊◊

Read the passages.

Romans 13:3-4
For rulers are not a terror to good conduct, but to bad. Would you have no fear of the one who is in authority? Then do what is good, and you will receive his approval, for he is God's servant for your good. But if you do wrong, be afraid, for he does not bear the sword in

vain. For he is the servant of God, an avenger who carries out God's wrath on the wrongdoer.

1 Timothy 2:1–2
First of all, then, I urge that supplications, prayers, intercessions, and thanksgivings be made for all people, for kings and all who are in high positions, that we may lead a peaceful and quiet life, godly and dignified in every way.

Analyze the passages.

What is the main emphasis in Romans 13:3-4 regarding the task of the civil government?

◊◊

For whom should we pray, according to Paul in 1 Timothy 2:1-2?

◊◊

Why does Paul urge his readers to pray for these people?

◊◊

What does 1 Timothy 2:1-2 suggest about the task of the civil government?

◊◊

Comments

Unfortunately, the Fall occurred, and that changes everything. Now we also need laws to protect people from each other and to combat the effects of sin. We need police and judges to make sure the laws are enforced and that justice is maintained. *This is the negative "mechanical" aspect of the development of society.*

This means that there are now two aspects of the *task* of the civil government, negative and positive. This is exactly what we find in the New Testament. Paul mentions the task of restraining evil in Romans 13. (Peter writes something similar in 1 Peter 2:13-14. He says the authorities of human institutions, including the emperor and his governors, are sent by God "to punish those who do evil and to praise those who do good.") Paul also says the rulers are God's servants "for your good." Then in 1 Timothy 2:1-2, he urges the readers to pray for all people, including "kings and all who are in high positions," so that we may lead a "peaceful and quiet life, godly and dignified in every way."

Notice the negative and positive aspects:
1) Rulers are a "terror" for wrongdoers and "bear the sword" to punish them.

2) Rulers are God's servants "for your good," and they should help you live a "peaceful and quiet life."

In order to restrain evil, they need to establish laws and enforce them. For example, the government establishes laws against stealing, then when someone robs another person, the authorities should punish him. The authorities also set speed limits and install stoplights to make the roads safe. When people disobey these guidelines and make things dangerous for others, they deserve to be punished.

Note that there is an exception to obeying the authorities. When they command you to do something against God's will, you should obey God first. Peter himself was one of the apostles that refused to stop preaching the gospel (Acts 4:19-20, 5:29).

Providing a "peaceful and quiet" environment points to *protecting freedom and maintaining peace and order.* Paul was especially concerned for the Christians who were being persecuted at the time he wrote 1 Timothy. But the phrase also suggests *maintaining peace and order* for legitimate activities in general.

To be "servants for your good" also includes the task of *maintaining peace and order*. The government needs to provide services that help society develop and function in a peaceful and orderly way. Some things can't be managed easily without the government, such as making sure people have water and electricity or building bridges and highways, for example. The government doesn't necessarily have to provide these things itself, but it needs to make sure somebody does. Many of these undertakings would have developed "organically," even without the presence of sin.

In summary, the main tasks of the civil government are to *restrain evil, protect freedom, and maintain peace and order*.

Notice that this description of the task of civil government doesn't imply that the government has the overarching task to manage every aspect of society or take care of every need. There are other institutions such as the Church and the family that also play an important role in caring for people.

In fact, the education of children is actually seen as the parents' responsibility in the Scriptures (Deuteronomy 6:6-7, Ephesians 6:4, Proverbs 22:6). This doesn't mean that it's necessarily wrong for the government to organize public schools or for Christian parents to send their children to public schools, but rather that they should stay informed about their children's education and discuss important topics with them. They should help them form a Christian worldview, just as we are proposing in this book. It also means that the government should allow families to do home-schooling and churches to organize private Christian schools.

The government should play the role of a *referee*. Normally he lets the athletes play freely, but he has to make sure they play by the rules and sanction them when they don't. In general, I would propose that the government should not interfere in the normal activities of people and institutions, except when some injustice or disorder exists between them. For example, the government shouldn't tell whether you should buy a mobile phone or where you should buy one. However, if you steal one from a store, you should be held accountable. Your "freedom" has become a lack of freedom for the store owner. As someone said, "My right to swing my arm ends where your nose begins."[5] Normally, the government should allow businesses to operate freely, but the moment the owners begin to abuse their workers or do something harmful or unjust, the government should step in to correct the situation.

For application

Do you agree with the comments about the task of the government? How would you describe its task? List some things you think the government should manage.

◊◊

◊◊

------

5 Several people have made similar statements, and it is not clear who first said it. <quoteinvestigator.com> "Your Liberty To Swing Your Fist Ends Just Where My Nose Begins" (Sept. 9, 2021)

Do you think the government should provide free health care for all citizens? How about free education? Explain your answer.

◊◊

◊◊

Take time to pray for your government rulers, starting with the president and his cabinet, then think of your state and local politicians. Write the names or offices of people that you pray for.

◊◊

◊◊

What other practical lessons can we learn from the passages studied in this lesson?

◊◊

4. The Covenant with Abraham

Genesis 12:1–3, Hebrews 11:9-16, Exodus 19:6

For previous reflection

How were the People of God first organized?

◊◊

When did they become organized as a "nation"?

◊◊

Read the passages.

Genesis 12:1–3
Now the LORD said to Abram, "Go from your country and your kindred and your father's house to the land that I will show you. And I will make of you a great nation, and I will bless you and make your name great, so that you will be a blessing. I will bless those who bless you, and him who dishonors you I will curse, and in you all the families of the earth shall be blessed."

Hebrews 11:9-10 and 16
By faith he went to live in the land of promise, as in a foreign land, living in tents with Isaac and Jacob, heirs with him of the same promise. For he was looking

forward to the city that has foundations, whose designer and builder is God.

...as it is, they desire a better country, that is, a heavenly one.

Exodus 19:6

...and you shall be to me a kingdom of priests and a holy nation.

Analyze the passages.

What did God ask Abram to do, according to Genesis 12:1-3?

◊◊

What did God promise Abram? List the blessings He promised.

◊◊

What other families did God promise to bless through Abram?

◊◊

According to Hebrews 11:9-10 and 16, what kind of city and what kind of country was Abram seeking?

◊◊

What did God call the Israelites after the exodus, according to Exodus 19:6?

◊◊

Comments

Israel had the privilege of being God's special People with whom God made His covenant during the period of the Old Testament. They began as a *family*, descendants of Abram (later called Abraham), a patriarchal tribe. God promised Abraham a people, a place, and His presence.

Later, after the exodus from Egypt, Israel became organized as a "holy nation," a "kingdom of priests," with laws to restrain the effects of sin (Exodus) and with a structure of appointed leaders (Numbers). Here they became what we call a "theocracy," in which God named the leaders and guided them directly. There was one official religion, the worship of Yahweh. Moses was a prophet, liberator, and ruler, but he served God as His direct representative. Upon entering the Promised Land, God raised up judges to rule over Israel (Judges 2:16).

However, the physical land of Canaan and the physical descendants of Abraham never were meant to be the main fulfillment of the covenant promises. The really important place was celestial and the people of God were to include families of believers from all over the earth.

For application
What can we learn from the promises made to Abram about the presence of God with His people? Do you think these promises apply to political nations now? Who receives the benefits of these promises now?

◊◊

What can we learn about the importance of a physical land for God's people now from Hebrews 11:9-10 and 16?

◊◊

What other practical lessons can we learn from the passages studied in this lesson?

◊◊

5. Israel's Monarchy in the Old Testament

Deuteronomy 17:14-15, 1 Samuel 8:7-18, 2 Chronicles 36:19-20

For previous reflection

Why did Old Testament Israel become a monarchy?

◊◊

Was it a good thing for them to become a monarchy?

◊◊

How did the monarchy end?

◊◊

Read the passages.

Deuteronomy 17:14-15
When you come to the land that the LORD your God is giving you, and you possess it and dwell in it and then say, "I will set a king over me, like all the nations that are around me," you may indeed set a king over you whom the LORD your God will choose.

1 Samuel 8:7-18

And the LORD *said to Samuel, "Obey the voice of the people in all that they say to you, for they have not rejected you, but they have rejected me from being king over them. ... Only you shall solemnly warn them and show them the ways of the king who shall reign over them." ...He said, "These will be the ways of the king who will reign over you: he will take your sons and appoint them to his chariots and to be his horsemen and to run before his chariots. And he will appoint for himself commanders of thousands and commanders of fifties, and some to plow his ground and to reap his harvest, and to make his implements of war and the equipment of his chariots. He will take your daughters to be perfumers and cooks and bakers. He will take the best of your fields and vineyards and olive orchards and give them to his servants. He will take the tenth of your grain and of your vineyards and give it to his officers and to his servants. He will take your male servants and female servants and the best of your young men and your donkeys, and put them to his work. He will take the tenth of your flocks, and you shall be his slaves. And in that day you will cry out because of your king, whom you have chosen for yourselves, but the* LORD *will not answer you in that day."*

2 Chronicles 36:19-20

And they burned the house of God and broke down the wall of Jerusalem and burned all its palaces with fire and destroyed all its precious vessels. He took into exile in Babylon those who had escaped from the sword, and they became servants to him and to his sons until the establishment of the kingdom of Persia.

Analyze the passages.

What did the Israelites ask for?

◊◊

Why did they ask for this? What did they want to become?

◊◊

Did God grant their request?

◊◊

Was God pleased with the fact that they made this request?

◊◊

What did Samuel warn the people about their future king? Mention some of the details.

◊◊

◊◊

According to 2 Chronicles 36:19-20, what happened when Babylon conquered Israel?

◊◊

Comments

The next stage of Israel's government after the time of the judges was a monarchy. Previously, while under the leadership of Moses, God had told them they would ask for a king one day and that their request would be granted (Deuteronomy 17:14-15).

Several centuries later, as was prophesied, they ask for a king "like all the nations" (1 Samuel 8:5). Here we read something curious: God grants their request, but He expresses discontent with the idea. God tells Samuel that they have rejected *Him* as their king (1 Samuel 8:7).

God also warns them through Samuel of the consequences of having such a king. He will send their sons out as soldiers, running before his chariots. He will put them to work making weapons and cultivating crops. He will "appoint for himself" military commanders and send others to plow "his" ground. He will call their daughters to be perfumers, cooks, and bakers. He will demand a tenth of their crops and their flocks, and they will be his "slaves" (1 Samuel 8:10-17). They will not be happy with this arrangement (1 Samuel 8:18).

But even after this warning, the people still ask for a king to judge over them and lead them into battle, "like all the nations" (v. 20). God tells Samuel to grant their request, even though it was wrong of them. Surely the motive to be "like all the nations" was offensive to Him. It was like "serving other gods" (v. 8). Nevertheless, He lets them have a king.

Why? We know that sometimes God grants our inappropriate requests in order to teach us a lesson. In this case, it would make them aware that it's not such a good idea to be like the other nations. They were supposed to be different!

This is also an example of something we see all through Scripture: God allows things that seem bad at the time, then turns them into something good. The best example is the crucifixion of Jesus; it was the worst sin ever committed, but it accomplished our salvation. In the case of letting Israel have a king "like the other nations," it was wrong of them to ask for this, but God turned it into something good: He prepared His people to live under secular rulers, to function as the salt of the earth among all nations.

From the beginning, God's plan always was to disperse His people throughout the world to bring positive change. God promised Abraham that all the families of the world would be blessed in him (Genesis 12:2-3). To accomplish this, His people would need to be weaned away from a theocracy. Eventually, God's people would not only have a king like the "other nations"; they would actually be *living* in these "other nations."

The period of the monarchy was not completely bad, especially under David and Solomon. However, the nation became   corrupt, with many evil kings and constant violence, then suffered a tragic division.

Finally, they were defeated by foreign nations and taken into exile. They lost their identity as a monarchy, having no king of their own. The Babylonians carried away king Zedekiah in chains, burned the temple, burned the palace, and broke down the walls of Jerusalem (2 Kings 25, 2 Chronicles 36).

Some of them later returned to Jerusalem and rebuilt the walls and the temple, but it was not like before. They suffered under the dominion of several different empires, including the Romans who were ruling at the time of Christ.

What does this brief historical sketch of the monarchy teach us? It clearly points to the need for salvation and to the need for Jesus as the perfect King. But what does it teach us about politics?

First, it teaches us that God uses governments to accomplish His purposes, but they will inevitably be imperfect and corrupt. In fact, the ideal government will never be established in this fallen world; we will have to wait until Christ returns. Meanwhile, like Abraham, we live "as in a foreign land," "looking forward to the city that has foundations, whose designer and builder is God." We desire a "better country, a heavenly one" (Hebrews 11:8-16).

Secondly, since the time of the exile, God's special covenant people is no longer a political nation or an ethnic group. God de-centralized His people and left them without a king. They only had prophets, priests, and elders. But this actually extended their realm of influence. Synagogues were established in different countries throughout the Mediterranean area, which eventually became platforms for preaching the Christian gospel message.

For application

What can we learn from these passages about how we should ask for things in prayer?

◊◊

Do you think any country can claim the privilege of being God's special People today? How about modern Israel? How about the United States? Explain your answer.

◊◊

What can we learn from the passages we analyzed in this lesson about the importance of the land that was once Old Testament Israel?

◊◊

Do you think Christians should try to form a world-wide organization with their own rulers?

◊◊

Do you see some of the same problems with modern day governments that Israel had during their monarchy? Give an example.

◊◊

What other practical lessons can we learn from the passages studied in this lesson?

◊◊

6. WHO ARE THE PEOPLE OF GOD NOW?

Matthew 28:19, Romans 9:8, Ephesians 3:6, Revelation 5:9-10

For previous reflection

If the nation of Israel is no longer the special People of God, how would you identify the People of God now?

◊◊

Read the passages.

Matthew 28:19
Go therefore and make disciples of all nations, baptizing them in the name of the Father and of the Son and of the Holy Spirit.

Romans 9:8
This means that it is not the children of the flesh who are the children of God, but the children of the promise are counted as offspring.

Ephesians 3:6
...The Gentiles are fellow heirs, members of the same body, and partakers of the promise in Christ Jesus through the gospel.

Revelation 5:9–10

...By your blood you ransomed people for God from every tribe and language and people and nation, and you have made them a kingdom and priests to our God, and they shall reign on the earth.

Analyze the passages.

From what "nations" (or ethnic groups) did Jesus command His followers to make disciples?

◊◊

Who are considered "children of God" now?

◊◊

What ethnic groups now belong to the Body of Christ?

◊◊

What have the ransomed people become?

◊◊

Where will these saved people eventually reign?

◊◊

Comments

The special People of God is no longer the political nation of Israel. When their Messiah came, the Jews rejected Him. Pilate asked them, "Shall I crucify your King?", and the chief priests answered, "We have no king but Caesar" (John 19:15). Then Pilate turned Jesus over to be crucified. Paul explains that the Jews "stumbled" over Jesus (Romans 9:30-33). Jesus had warned them that the kingdom would be taken away from them (Matthew 21:43).

Now there is "neither Jew nor Greek" (Galatians 3:28); all believers are united in Christ (Ephesians 2:11-22). Jesus died to ransom people "from every tribe and language and people and nation" (Revelation 5:9). The fact that the Gentiles are included is a prominent theme in the New Testament. Similar to events like the Great Flood and the Exodus, it is a historical dramatization of the gospel, the message of reconciliation. All the people who are saved belong to the kingdom of God, they are "priests to God," and they will eventually reign on the new earth (Revelation 5:10).

This has important practical implications today. It means that *no country and no ethnic group can claim the privilege of being God's special chosen People now.* God's people, as Christians, are spread throughout the world in ALL political nations.

The people of God are not any one nation,
but they are *in* all nations.

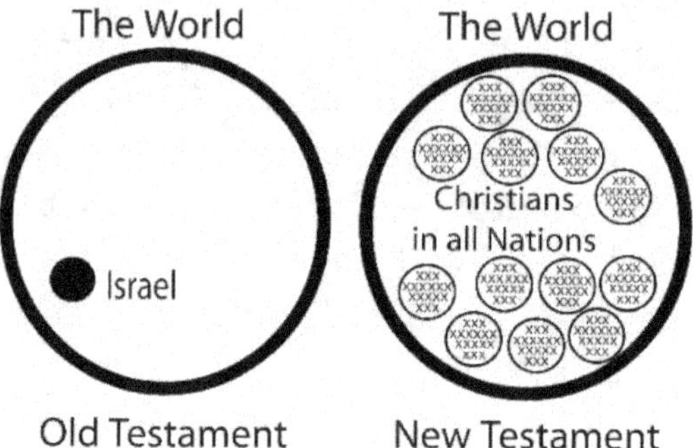

It also means that God condemns all forms of racism and prejudice. Think of the perverse manifestations of hateful discrimination within the last centuries such as slavery and the persecution of the Jews. Even today, "white supremacy" is a dangerous growing force.

For application

How should the theological principle that God's special People is no longer one political nation change your attitude toward other nations and their people?

◊◊

When does a healthy sense of patriotism become an unhealthy attitude toward other countries? Give an example.

◊◊

Some Christians believe that the modern nation of Israel is still the special People of God today. What would you say to them about that now? What difference does this make?

◊◊

How have you seen racism and prejudice evident in your lifetime?

◊◊

How do you think we should treat foreigners who come to our country?

◊◊

Do you sometimes struggle with attitudes of racism or prejudice?

◊◊

7. SENT INTO THE WORLD

John 17:15-18, Jeremiah 29:4-7

For previous reflection

Do you think Christians should be involved in politics? If so, in what way? Give an example.

◊◊

Read the passages.

John 17:15–18
I do not ask that you take them out of the world, but that you keep them from the evil one. They are not of the world, just as I am not of the world. Sanctify them in the truth; your word is truth. As you sent me into the world, so I have sent them into the world.

Jeremiah 29:4-7
Thus says the LORD of hosts, the God of Israel, to all the exiles whom I have sent into exile from Jerusalem to Babylon: Build houses and live in them; plant gardens and eat their produce. Take wives and have sons and daughters; take wives for your sons, and give your daughters in marriage, that they may bear sons and daughters; multiply there, and do not decrease. But seek the welfare of the city where I have sent you into exile,

and pray to the LORD on its behalf, for in its welfare you will find your welfare.

Analyze the passages.

What does Jesus pray for in the first sentence of John 17:15?

◊◊

What do you think Jesus means when He says, "they are not of the world"?

◊◊

What do you think He means when He says, "As you sent Me into the world, so I have sent them into the world"? What does this tell us about how Christians should relate to the world around us, to society and culture?

◊◊

◊◊

How were the Israelites supposed to live when they were exiles in Babylon? Mention some examples.

◊◊

Comments

When I was in college, students were protesting on campus against war and speaking against racism. Then I would go to church on Sunday where our topics of discussion always seemed far removed from what was really happening in the "real world." For a while I thought (wrongly, of course) that the church was not going to make much difference in the world.

There have been different views throughout history of how Christians should relate to society and culture, including politics. We'll look at three basic positions.[6]

1. We should separate from the world.

Defenders of this position emphasize the presence of sin in society and tend to separate themselves from the "world." Some live in monasteries to avoid sinful society and worldly cares. Others live in their own separate communities and refuse to drive cars, watch television, or use electricity. Some churches have a policy of "Do not smoke, drink, dance, or go to movies, and *do not be friends with anyone who does.*" I know people who only read Christian books or listen to Christian songs.

---

[6] My main source for studying this issue is Richard H. Niebuhr, *Christ and Culture*, (Harper and Row, New York, 1975), which is considered a classic study. He explains five different positions. To simplify, we will consider only three main outlooks.

2. We should join the world.

These people believe that Christ is operating in and through culture, and they minimize the effects of sin. They think we should cooperate with the current cultural tendencies, instead of fighting against them or running from them. Richard Niebuhr calls them "cultural Christians."[7] One example is the tendency in the first few centuries after Jesus to mix oriental religion and Greek philosophy with Christianity. More recently, Liberation theology reflected a similar attitude, trying to combine Marxism with Christianity.

3. We should transform the world.

Representatives of this concept believe that culture is basically evil, but that the grace of God is present too, bringing positive transformation. We should not separate ourselves from the world nor go along with it. Instead, we should stay in it and work toward changing it. Jeremiah exhorted the exiles in Babylon to build houses, to plant gardens, to "seek the welfare" of that city and to pray for it, "for in its welfare you will find your welfare" (Jeremiah 29:4-7). John Calvin expressed this view, not only in his writings, but in his life, especially in Geneva. He labored for years to convert the city into a model Christian society. Although they made mistakes, they did a lot of good things: they received refugees, took care of the sick and the elderly, transformed the laws of commerce, and even constructed a sewage system. They literally cleaned up the city!

---

[7] Niebuhr, p. 106

This position seems to fit the concept of being *in* the world, but not *of* the world, as Jesus prayed for the disciples. It also enables us to reflect the image of God, who is creative and fixes what is broken. Finally, it fulfills the "cultural mandate" taught in Genesis 1:26-28, as we studied in lesson 2.

For application

Which of the three positions explained in the comments describes you best? How can you practice being *in* the world but not *of* the world? Give an example.

◊◊

◊◊

How would you apply John 17:15-18 to your involvement in politics? Give an example.

◊◊

What can we learn from Jeremiah 29:4-7 about living under secular governments?

◊◊

8. Politics and the Kingdom of God

John 18:36, Acts 1:6-8

For previous reflection

How would you describe the kingdom of God? How is it established?

◊◊

What do you think the kingdom of God has to do with politics?

◊◊

Read the passages.

John 18:36
Jesus answered, "My kingdom is not of this world. If my kingdom were of this world, my servants would have been fighting, that I might not be delivered over to the Jews. But my kingdom is not from the world."

Acts 1:6-8
So when they had come together, they asked him, "Lord, will you at this time restore the kingdom to Israel?" He said to them, "It is not for you to know times or seasons that the Father has fixed by his own authority.

But you will receive power when the Holy Spirit has come upon you, and you will be my witnesses in Jerusalem and in all Judea and Samaria, and to the end of the earth."

Analyze the passages.

What do you think Jesus meant when He said, "My kingdom is not of this world"?

◊◊

What did the disciples ask Jesus in Acts 1:6-8? What do you think they meant? What do you think they were expecting at this time?

◊◊

How did Jesus answer?

◊◊

What do you think He meant with His answer?

◊◊

Comments

People often misunderstood the nature of Jesus' kingdom. Herod the Great tried to kill Him as a baby, because he was afraid He might eventually replace him as king over Judea (Matthew 2:1-12). Satan tempted

Jesus by offering Him "all the kingdoms of the world" if He would fall down and worship him, but Jesus rebuked him (Luke 4:4-8). When Pilate asked Him if He was king of the Jews, Jesus answered, "My kingdom is not of this world," then added, "if my kingdom were of this world, my servants would have been fighting, that I might not be delivered over to the Jews" (John 18:33-36).

Even the disciples misunderstood this. In Acts 1:6-8, they ask Him if He is going to restore the kingdom to Israel. They apparently expected Him to initiate a movement to end the oppression of the Romans and restore the nation of Israel to something like the monarchy under David. They were probably confused with His answer at first, when He said they would receive power from the Holy Spirit and would be His witnesses. Maybe they even thought He misunderstood them.

Is He saying that they shouldn't be concerned with the coming of the kingdom? Or that the only important thing now is evangelism? Of course not. It may have been hard for the disciples to comprehend at first, but He understood the question perfectly and He was actually explaining how the kingdom of God would be established.

It's not by force, not with weapons, not by establishing a powerful political nation, nor by making the Church a world-wide government, but by testifying about Jesus. The Holy Spirit was going to come with more power than ever, and He would take them to every corner of the world with the message. That's the way His kingdom will be established. The only way to bring true change to society is through a spiritual change in peoples' hearts.

But it doesn't end with conversion; that's just the beginning. The epicenter of change is the heart, but the effects ripple through the family, the church, and all of society, including politics, social media, business, education, science, medical care, art, literature, ...everything. As God reigns in the heart, every aspect of a person's way of thinking and living is transformed. Jesus taught the disciples to pray, "Your kingdom come, your will be done, on earth as it is in heaven" (Matthew 6:10). When God's will is done, His kingdom comes.

For example, suppose that a very selfish man is the owner of a shoe factory, in which he doesn't pay his workers a fair wage or treat them with respect. The only thing he wants to do is make more money. The workers can protest and plead with him to be fair, but he won't care. However, if he becomes a Christian, his attitude will change, then he will pay them better and treat them better. This is the coming of the kingdom!

A secretary glorifies God, not only by being nice to her colleagues or by sharing the Good News with them (without denying the importance of these things), but also while carrying out her regular tasks, however tedious and insignificant they may seem at the moment. Why? Because she is manifesting the image of God and because her work benefits society. It's a way to fulfill the cultural mandate and extend the kingdom of God.

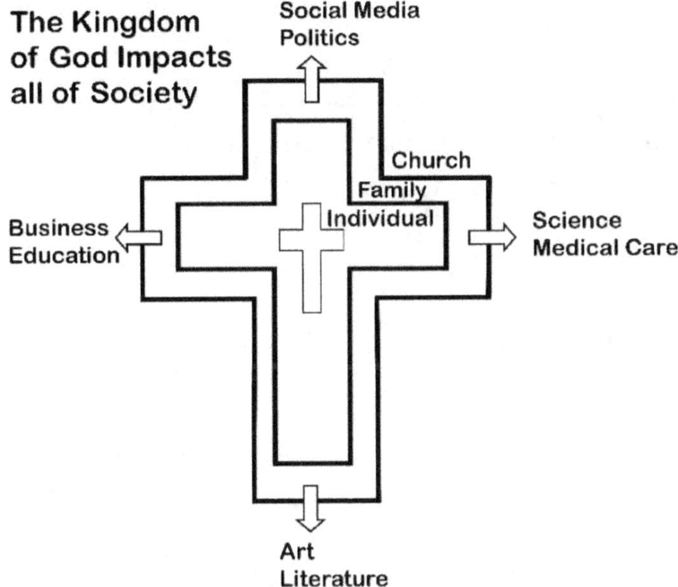

The kingdom of God cannot be identified with any political movement, and God's special instrument for establishing His kingdom is not politics. Instead, it's the power of the Holy Spirit transforming people through the preaching of the gospel, who in turn transform the world around them.

However, this doesn't mean politics are insignificant, or that the civil government is no concern of ours. *The kingdom of God permeates the world of politics, just as it transforms all areas of society.*

The Kingdom of God is not *of* this world,
but it *transforms* the world.

For application

In what ways have you observed the kingdom of God manifesting its presence in your personal life or in the life of others around you?

◊◊

In what ways have you observed the kingdom of God manifesting its presence in the *political* world?

◊◊

Do you know people who believe that the kingdom of God can be identified with a *country* or with a political movement today? How would you respond to them?

◊◊

What do you think of the following comment by Richard John Neuhaus?: "The first thing to say about politics is that politics is not the first thing."[8]

◊◊

---

[8] Nathaniel Peters, "Time Toward Home: Richard John Neuhaus for Our Time" <https://www.thepublicdiscourse.com/2024/01/92321/>, Jan.7, 2024.

9. RENDER TO CAESAR; A LESSON FROM A COIN

Matthew 22:15–22

For previous reflection

How do you think Christians should relate to their civil government? Should they also submit to corrupt or oppressive regimes? Is there ever a time to disobey?

◊◊

◊◊

Read the passage.

Matthew 22:15–22

Then the Pharisees went and plotted how to entangle him in his words. And they sent their disciples to him, along with the Herodians, saying, "Teacher, we know that you are true and teach the way of God truthfully, and you do not care about anyone's opinion, for you are not swayed by appearances. Tell us, then, what you think. Is it lawful to pay taxes to Caesar, or not?" But Jesus, aware of their malice, said, "Why put me to the test, you hypocrites? Show me the coin for the tax." And they brought him a denarius. And Jesus said to them, "Whose likeness and inscription is this?" They said, "Caesar's." Then he said to them, "Therefore render to

Caesar the things that are Caesar's, and to God the things that are God's." When they heard it, they marveled. And they left him and went away.

Analyze the passage.

In what way do you think the Pharisees and Herodians were trying to test Jesus?

◊◊

What did they ask Him?

◊◊

How did Jesus answer?

◊◊

What do you think He meant?

◊◊

Comments

How should Christians relate to their civil government? We should apply the "transformation" principle that we studied previously regarding culture and society in general. That is, instead of staying away or going along with the secular influence, we should work to transform our government to make it better.

Political efforts don't change people much, but people can change politics a lot.

When the Pharisees and Herodians asked Jesus if it was lawful to pay taxes to Caesar (Matthew 22:15-22), He asked them to show Him a coin and answered them with another question: "Whose likeness and inscription is this?" When they answered that it was Caesar's image on the coin, He wisely replied, "Therefore render to Caesar the things that are Caesar's and to God the things that are God's."

They were trying to trap Him. On the one hand, the Herodians were supporters of Rome and would consider it illegal to refuse to pay taxes. On the other hand, the Pharisees hated Rome and would consider it offensive and immoral to support Caesar. They thought they had Him cornered, but they didn't.

How did Jesus outwit them? Notice that He doesn't say that they should refuse to pay taxes to such a pagan government or that they should overthrow the Roman Empire. But neither does He allow them to think that they can recognize Caesar as their highest authority. Notice that neither the Herodians nor the Pharisees were able to criticize His answer; they were amazed and went away.

Jesus doesn't mean they should keep these two aspects of their lives totally separate, as if to say, "follow the government rules for *secular* matters and follow

God's rules for *spiritual* matters." He's not suggesting that there are two separate kingdoms.

So what does Jesus mean? He is putting things in their proper place. If the coin has the image of Caesar, it belongs to him. But Caesar has the image of God on his person, and therefore Caesar belongs to God! Jesus reminds them of the fact that God is sovereign over all things, including the Roman Empire.

Donald Carson explains that this passage doesn't warrant an "absolute dichotomy between God and Caesar, or between church and state, or between Christ and culture." He adds that "if we give back to God what has *his* image on it, we must all give ourselves to him. …We may be obligated to pay taxes to Caesar, but we owe everything, our very being, to God."[9]

Jesus is agreeing that it's legitimate to pay taxes to Caesar. Paul confirmed this in Romans 13. But He is teaching something more profound: you can live under a civil government, even a corrupt one, and fulfill civil duties like this, without betraying your commitment to God. This points again to the concept of being "in" the world to transform it, but not "of" the world. It also fits the plan for Christians to be dispersed and live under different kinds of civil governments in different countries.

But to do this requires being faithful to God above any worldly ruler. If the civil authorities require us to do something against God's will, we are obligated to refuse.

---

[9] Donald A. Carson, *Christ and Culture Revisited*. (Grand Rapids: Eerdmans, 2008), Kindle edition, p. 57.

When the authorities forbid the disciples to preach in the name of Jesus, they disobeyed in order to put God first (Acts 4:19, 5:29).

For application

Did this lesson change your view about how Christians should relate to their civil government? In what way?

◊◊

Give examples of ways in which you could have a positive influence in the government of your country.

◊◊

Give an example of a situation in which a Christian should disobey his civil government.

◊◊

10. HOW TO APPLY THE OT LAWS TODAY

2 Timothy 3:16, Hebrews 10:10-12, Romans 13:1, Acts 10:13-15

For previous reflection

Do you think we need to keep the Old Testament laws today in the same way they were supposed to keep them in Old Testament Israel? Why or why not?

◊◊

Do you think our governments should punish people today in the same way Old Testament Israel was supposed to?

◊◊

Read the Passages:

2 Timothy 3:16
All Scripture is breathed out by God and profitable for teaching, for reproof, for correction, and for training in righteousness.

Hebrews 10:10-12
...We have been sanctified through the offering of the body of Jesus Christ once for all. And every priest

stands daily at his service, offering repeatedly the same sacrifices, which can never take away sins. But when Christ had offered for all time a single sacrifice for sins, he sat down at the right hand of God.

Romans 13:1

Let every person be subject to the governing authorities. For there is no authority except from God, and those that exist have been instituted by God.

Acts 10:13-15

And there came a voice to him: "Rise, Peter; kill and eat." But Peter said, "By no means, Lord; for I have never eaten anything that is common or unclean." And the voice came to him again a second time, "What God has made clean, do not call common."

Analyze the passages

According to 2 Timothy 3:16, what parts of Scripture teach us moral guidelines for our spiritual lives?

◊◊

According to Hebrews 10:10-12 what is the difference between the Old Testament priestly sacrifices and the sacrifice that Jesus made?

◊◊

According to Romans 13:1, should we obey the laws of pagan governments? Why?

◊◊

According to Acts 10:13–15, should we obey the same Old Testament prohibitions regarding "unclean" food?

◊◊

Comments

There's an important issue to address as we consider how to influence our government for better laws: how should we apply the laws of the Old Testament today? I often witness confusion regarding this matter. I cringe when a pastor is interviewed on TV and doesn't know what to say when the reporter asks him about the Old Testament punishments for certain kinds of immoral behavior.

Some theologians believe that we should apply the laws of the Old Testament now in basically the same way as in the ancient times, and that we should try to influence our governments to establish laws for that purpose.[10] On the other extreme are those who believe that the laws of the Old Testament have no application at all for us today; they were only for the Jews during the Old Testament.[11]

———————————

[10] See, for example, Greg Bahnsen, *Theonomy in Christian Ethics* (Nutley, N.J.: Craig Press, 1979), p.73.
[11] See for example Lewis Sperry Chafer, *Systematic Theology*, 8 vols. (Dallas: Dallas Seminary Press, 1948) 4:166, 208-210.

John Calvin proposed a more balanced solution. He made a distinction between three aspects of the Old Testament law: the ceremonial aspect, the civil aspect, and the moral aspect. It's not that different verses fit neatly into different categories; the three aspects overlap. These laws still teach us important truths, but the applications changed in the time of the New Testament.

Since Jesus made the last sacrifice (Hebrews 9:24-28, 10:11-14), we do not have to keep the *ceremonial* aspect of the law. That is, we no longer make sacrifices, and we no longer observe the rituals and ceremonies related to the temple. A change regarding forbidden foods is manifested when Peter sees a vision with all kinds of animals and a voice from heaven tells him that he is free to eat them (Acts 10:13-15 and 11:5-10).

In a similar way, since the People of God is no longer one political nation (Israel), but rather believers from all nations, we no longer need to keep the *civil* aspect of the law as they did before Christ. This aspect was related especially to things like the stipulated punishments and the management of properties. For example, we no longer are required to punish adultery or homosexual relations by death (Leviticus 20:10,13). There were laws related to properties that we no longer need to observe, such as the Year of Jubilee (Leviticus 25), in which property was to return to its original owner every fifty years, Hebrew prisoners were to be set free, and debts were to be cancelled. Now we are called to submit to the authorities of the government we are living under

(Romans 13:1). In the sermon on the mount (Matthew 5-7), Jesus radically changed the Old Testament perspective on ethical principles, focusing more on the heart motives and less on the physical details of the actions, offering more grace and less legalism.

However, the *moral* aspect of the law should still be observed as in the Old Testament period. These universal ethical principles reflect the character of God, and are for all people in all times. Although we don't need to observe the details of the civil laws, they still contain lessons for us regarding *general principles of justice*. For example, stealing is still a sin and being selfish with our material possessions is still a sin. Furthermore, while we don't need to observe the details of the ceremonial laws either, they still teach us *spiritual truths*. For example, the sacrifices point to the sacrifice of Jesus on the cross. In other words, we do not apply the civil and ceremonial laws in the same way that they were supposed to back then, but we can find helpful teachings in them.[12] The *Westminster Confession of Faith* also makes this three-way distinction (chapter 19).

---

[12] John Calvin, *Institutes of the Christian Religion,* (IV,20,15). See also *Commentaries on the Four Last Books of Moses Arranged in the Form of a Harmony,* trans. Charles William Bingham, 4 volumes (Edinburgh: The Calvin Translation Society, 1843) 1:498-502.

Three Aspects of the O.T. Law

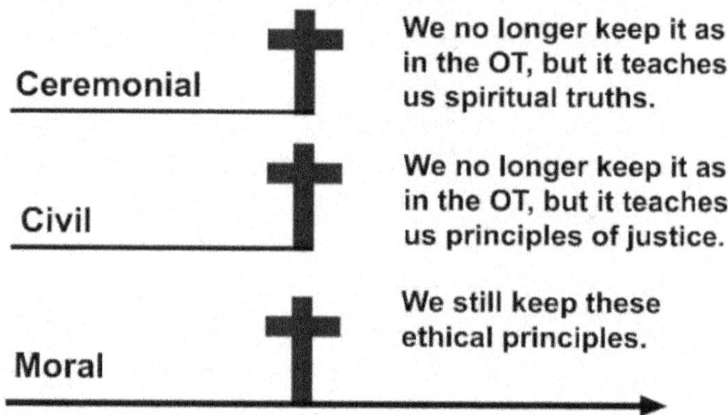

This changes the way we should try to influence the laws of our civil government. We shouldn't ask the government to apply the civil aspects or the ceremonial aspects of the law in the way required in the Old Testament.

For application

Did this lesson change your view of how we should apply the laws of the Old Testament now? Give an example.

◊◊

What application can we make from the Old Testament commandment to return all land to its original owner every fifty years (Leviticus 25)?

◊◊

What application can we make from the Old Testament ceremony of sacrificing a lamb every year during Passover (Exodus 12)?

◊◊

Give another example of a moral principle we can learn from the Old Testament civil laws or ceremonial laws, without applying them in the same way as they were supposed to at that time.

◊◊

11. Biblical Principles for the Economy

Proverbs 11:1, Proverbs 6:6–9, Leviticus 23:22

For previous reflection

What are some biblical principles you would recommend that your government put into practice for a good economic policy?

◊◊

Read the passages.

Proverbs 11:1
A false balance is an abomination to the LORD, but a just weight is his delight.

Proverbs 6:6-9
Go to the ant, O sluggard; consider her ways, and be wise. Without having any chief, officer, or ruler, she prepares her bread in summer and gathers her food in harvest. How long will you lie there, O sluggard? When will you arise from your sleep?

Leviticus 23:22
And when you reap the harvest of your land, you shall not reap your field right up to its edge, nor shall you gather the gleanings after your harvest. You shall leave

them for the poor and for the sojourner: I am the LORD your God.

Analyze the passages.

What ethical principle is taught in Proverbs 11:1?

◊◊

What ethical principle is taught in Proverbs 6:6-9?

◊◊

What ethical principle is taught in Leviticus 23:22?

◊◊

Comments

We find three general ethical guidelines for economics highlighted in the Old Testament that should help us develop a good economic philosophy: be honest, work diligently and show compassion.

The principle of honesty permeates the whole Old Testament. The ninth commandment is "You shall not bear false witness against your neighbor" (Exodus 20:16). Proverbs 11:1 says, "A false balance is an abomination to the Lord, but a just weight is His delight."

The Book of Proverbs emphasizes the wisdom of working hard and being honest (6:6-11, 16:11, 19:1, 20:4, 24:27, 26:13-14). Proverbs 30:8-9 teaches that it is better to be neither extremely wealthy nor extremely poor, because wealth tends to make us think we don't need God, but poverty tempts us to steal.

The Pentateuch, in passages such as Leviticus 25, teach us that we are free to make an effort to improve our situation, but that we must show compassion to the needy. During 50 years, you could work hard, farm more land, and earn more for your family. But after 50 years, all the land went back to the original owner. This put a limit on how long you could build up more and more for yourself. Without limits like this, one person would eventually end up owning everything!

There were many provisions made for the poor, such as leaving part of the crop unharvested so that they could find something to eat (Leviticus 23:22). Nobody should have starved to death in Israel! The story of manna in the desert (Exodus 16:16-31) illustrates several principles. Those who gathered much had just enough, and those who gathered little also had enough, which teaches us to avoid selfish excess. Those who tried to keep manna overnight found that it had been spoiled by morning, which teaches us to trust God daily for our provision.

The prophets emphasized showing compassion and treating the needy with justice. They announced punishment for "trampling the head of the poor into the dust of the earth" and "turning aside the way of the afflicted" (Amos 2:7). They scolded Israel for mistreating the foreigners, orphans, and widows (Jeremiah 7:6).

These three Old Testament ethical principles of honesty, diligence and compassion make a perfect harmony. Putting them into practice would establish a healthy and fair economy.

As for the New Testament, Jesus inculcated new ethical values and new attitudes. We are not to lay up treasures on earth (Matthew 6:19-20), neither are we to be anxious about material things, but trust our heavenly Father (Matthew 6:25-34). Wealth can make it difficult to see the need for God, and therefore difficult to enter the Kingdom of God (Matthew 19:23). We should give to the poor, even be willing to give up everything if necessary (Luke 18:18-30). Jesus Himself gave us an example of sacrificing our own comfort to help others.

2 Corinthians 8:9

For you know the grace of our Lord Jesus Christ, that though He was rich, yet for your sake He became poor, so that you through His poverty might become rich.

God has a special concern for those who are in need, whether it is someone who is depressed, who lives in a broken family, who is struggling with drugs, who lives far from home, or who is poor in material possessions. If we were to practice the values that Jesus left us, and if we were to have the attitude that Jesus had toward those who are suffering, the economy would be much better.

In Acts 2:44-45 and 4:32-34, it is evident that the church of the first century practiced the principles that Jesus had taught. They sold their possessions and shared with those in need, with the result that "there were no needy persons among them" (Acts 4:34). Some consider this a sort of "communist" experiment. However, the sharing was voluntary, the result of "much grace" being upon them (Acts 4:33). We see the same attitude in Paul, when he encourages the Corinthians to seek greater equality, following the guideline of the manna in the desert (2 Corinthians 8:14-15), but asks them to give out of grace, following the example of Christ, and not out of obligation (8:8-9).

The New Testament certainly doesn't encourage laziness or passivity. 2 Thessalonians 3:10 gives us a guideline: "If anyone is not willing to work, then he is not to eat either." But it does encourage us to be content with what we have. Paul says, "I know how to get along with humble means, and I also know how to live in prosperity" (Philippians 4:12; see also 1 Timothy 6:8 and Hebrews 13:5). I can testify to the fact that good relationships and a grateful attitude contribute more to happiness than material possessions.

Heinrich Böll writes a story about a happy fisherman and an annoying tourist. The fisherman had already gone to sea and had made his catch for the day, when a tourist comes along and wakes him from a nap with the clicking of his camera. They begin to talk, and the visitor tries to convince him that he should go back out again and catch more fish, in order to make more money and improve his business. The well-meaning visitor gets excited as he imagines how the poor man could eventually purchase more boats, build a factory, open a restaurant, and become very rich. "What then?", the unimpressed fisherman asks. "Then you may relax here in the harbor with your mind set at ease, doze in the sunshine and look out on the magnificent sea," the tourist argues. "But that is just what I am doing now!", says the fisherman.[13] This story illustrates the contrast between being eager to obtain more material possessions and learning to be content, an important lesson in our materialistic world.

For application

Give examples of how your government could put into practice the biblical principles mentioned in the passages we looked at.

◊◊

Give examples of how you personally could put into practice these principles.

◊◊

Can you think of other biblical teachings that should influence the economic policies of your government?

◊◊

---

[13] Heinrich Böll, *Anekdote zur Senkung der Arbeitsmoral* ["Anecdote to the Decline of the Work Ethic"] There are many versions of this story, often without citing the source.< https://en.wikipedia.org/wiki/Anekdote_zur_Senkung_der_Arbeitsmoral>

ADDITIONAL READINGS

12. What is the Best Form of Government?

There are different ways to categorize forms of government, and it can be confusing, because some of them overlap. The following are important terms to help classify governments: [14]

Monarchy: Throughout history, including Bible history, most governments have been monarchies. This means either a king or queen inherits the right to rule by being next in line of succession within the royal family. In an absolute monarchy, the ruler has power over everything, but in many monarchies, the power is limited by a constitution or by other branches of the government.

Republic: In a republic, the power to rule rests in the people, who elect representatives to govern, following the guidelines of a constitution, and they do not have a king or queen.

Democracy: This also refers to a system of government in which the power rests in the people. There are basically two kinds: a) In a "representative democracy," the people elect representatives to make decisions for them. While some make a distinction, for our purposes in this book, we will consider "representative democracy" synonymous with a "republic." Over half the nations of the world today fit this description. b) In a "direct democracy," people vote

---

[14] See <https://www.merriam-webster.com/dictionary>

directly on all issues, instead of electing representatives to make decisions for them.

Dictatorship: In this form of government, one person or a small group of people has absolute power. In contrast with a typical monarchy today, the power to rule in a dictatorship is obtained by force and is exercised by force, as in a military dictatorship for example.

Totalitarianism: This term describes the extent of power exercised by the ruler or rulers. It means they intend to control every aspect of society, including the media and the economy, leaving little personal freedom, and using repressive means to accomplish it. This could take the form of a dictatorship, but it could also take the form of a government ruled by just one party.

Which is best?

Considering the power of sin and selfishness, a government that includes a constitution, a system of checks and balances, and a wider sharing of the power to make decisions, like a republic or representative democracy, is normally better. Furthermore, after considering the task of the civil government, it seems wise to keep their power limited and guarantee a healthy amount of personal freedom. Totalitarianism is dangerous. However, we should also be careful not to assume we know exactly how these principles should be applied in contexts and cultures that we don't know or understand.

13. Church and State; A Brief Summary

The question of how the Church should relate to the civil government has been debated throughout history (often expressed in terms of the relation between "Church and State.") Does the government have authority over the Church? Does the Church have authority over the government? Should there be a "wall of separation" between them? We will provide a brief historical overview, focusing on the Christian Church in the countries of the Western world.

During the first few centuries after Christ, Christians in the Roman Empire were persecuted for their religious beliefs and practices, or tolerated at best. They were often punished because they refused to worship the roman gods and the emperor. Under Constantine, Christianity was legalized (the Edict of Milan, 313) and became protected by the emperor. He had the authority to organize the Council of Nicaea in 325 to resolve theological issues. In 380, Christianity became the official religion of the Roman Empire (The Edict of Thessalonica).

During the following centuries, the Church became a powerful institution that had a very close relationship with the civil government. Normally the government had the upper hand, but sometimes the Church did. The Church seemed to have authority over the state when they initiated the Crusades (1095) and called on the civil leaders to carry out the battles. However, in other cases like Spain, the monarchy exercised authority over religious matters. The inquisition in Spain (beginning in

1478) was established to preserve their Catholic beliefs and punish Jews, Muslims, and later also Protestants. The Spanish government soon forced their religion on the indigenous people that they conquered in the Americas.

During the time of the Reformation and the subsequent Counter-Reformation, the common assumption was that the civil government would decide the religious identity of its territory. Protestants and Catholics struggled to gain dominion over the independent states of the Holy Roman Empire, leading to wars and persecution. An estimated 8 million people died in the *Thirty Years' War* in Europe between 1618 and 1648.[15] England also suffered a period of wars until they adopted Anglicanism as their official state religion, situation that continues to this day.

John Calvin was beginning to discern a solution to this problem, but he wasn't totally consistent. He proposed that the civil magistrates govern the matters of "outward morality," and that the Church govern the affairs of "inner man."[16] However, when Calvin speaks of the task of the civil government, he includes the prevention of blasphemy and religious offenses. This contradicts his distinction, because these are matters of the "inner man." Furthermore, he agreed with the city

---

[15] See <https://www.britannica.com/event/Thirty-Years-War> and <https://www.history.com/articles/thirty-years-war>.
[16] *Institutes*, IV, XX, 1.

council in Geneva when they sentenced Michael Servetus to death for holding a heretical view of the Trinity.[17]

In 1646, his followers in England drafted *The Westminster Confession of Faith*. They proposed that the civil government should not "interfere in matters of faith" or establish a preferred denomination, but protect the Church and guarantee its freedom.

> Civil magistrates may not assume to themselves the administration of the Word and sacraments; or the power of the keys of the kingdom of heaven; yet he has authority, and it is his duty to take order that unity and peace be preserved in the Church, ...

> Yet, as nursing fathers, it is the duty of civil magistrates to protect the Church of our common Lord, without giving the preference to any denomination of Christians above the rest, in such a manner that all ecclesiastical persons whatever shall enjoy the full, free, and unquestioned liberty of discharging every part of their sacred functions, without violence or danger.[18]

However, similar to Calvin, they still didn't limit the authority of the government clearly. According to the early versions of the *Confession*, the civil magistrate even had authority to supervise ecclesiastical councils,

---

[17] "Why did John Calvin have Michael Servetus burned at the stake for heresy?" Got Questions.<https://www.gotquestions.org/Calvin-Michael-Servetus.html> (March 14, 2026).

[18] *Westminster Confession of Faith,* Chapter 23, section 3. Version of 1646.

suppress religious error and prevent abuse in worship. He should guarantee…

> …that the truth of God be kept pure and entire, that all blasphemies and heresies be suppressed, all corruptions and abuses in worship and discipline prevented or reformed, and all the ordinances of God duly settled, administrated, and observed. For the better effecting whereof, he has power to call synods, to be present at them and to provide that whatsoever is transacted in them be according to the mind of God.[19]

A later American version of the *Westminster Confession* in 1788 took out the section quoted above regarding suppressing heresies and abuses in worship, as well as the right to call synods. They made it very clear that the government should not "in the least interfere in matters of faith." Read the same section quoted above after it was modified in the version of 1788:

> Civil magistrates may not assume to themselves the administration of the Word and sacraments; or the power of the keys of the kingdom of heaven; *or, in the least, interfere in matters of faith*. Yet, as nursing fathers, it is the duty of civil magistrates to protect the church of our common Lord, without giving the preference to any denomination of

---

[19] *Westminster Confession of Faith*, Ch. 23, section 3. Version of 1646. <https://www.blueletterbible.org/study/ccc/westminster/Of_The_Civil_Magistrate.cfm> (Feb. 27, 2026)

Christians above the rest in such a manner, that all ecclesiastical persons whatever shall enjoy the full, free, and unquestioned liberty of discharging, every part of their sacred functions, without violence or danger. And, as Jesus Christ hath appointed a regular government and discipline in his church, no law of any commonwealth, should interfere with, let, or hinder, the due exercise thereof, among the voluntary members of any denomination of Christians, according to their own profession and belief. It is the duty of civil magistrates to protect the person and good name of all their people, in such an effectual manner as that no person be suffered, either upon pretense of religion or of infidelity, to offer any indignity, violence, abuse, or injury to any other person whatsoever: and to take order, that all religious and ecclesiastical assemblies be held without molestation or disturbance.[20]

This perspective was important for the United States, where many people had come seeking freedom of religion and where there existed a variety of religious tendencies. Thomas Jefferson wrote of the "wall of separation" between religion and the government. The First Amendment of the constitution says the following:

---

[20] The 1788 American Revision of the Westminster Standards, p. 10. *Westminster Confession of Faith*, chapter 23, section 3. <Microsoft Word - 1788_revision.doc (upper-register.com)>, (Oct. 18, 2023).

Congress shall make no law respecting an establishment of religion, or prohibiting the free exercise thereof; or abridging the freedom of speech, or of the press; or the right of the people peaceably to assemble, and to petition the Government for a redress of grievances.[21]

The relation between Church and State has continued to be a complicated subject in many countries. When the Latin American countries were colonized, most began with Roman Catholicism as the official state religion, but almost all eventually changed their constitutions to eliminate the policy of an official religion. However, the Catholic Church still enjoys special privileges. In Europe, the situation is similar; a few countries still have an official religion, but they all permit freedom for others. For example, Denmark recognizes the Lutheran Church as the established church, England recognizes the Anglican Church, and Greece recognizes the Orthodox Church.[22] Other countries give special privileges to a particular church, without considering it the official state religion. For example, the Catholic Church is still predominant in Spain. Germany and France consider themselves "neutral" with regard to religion.

This brief historical sketch demonstrates that it's not a good idea for either the Church to have authority over the State or for the State to have authority over the

---

[21] "The Constitution Annotated,"
<https://constitution.congress.gov/constitution/amendment-1> (July 1, 2010).
[22] "State Religion" in *Wikipedia*: <http://en.wikipedia.org/wiki/State_religion> (July 1, 2010).

Church. While there are exceptions, having a state religion tends to lead to unfair treatment of minority groups, even to persecution. However, the image of a "wall of separation" isn't the best metaphor to explain the proper relationship between them. Such a phrase sounds like neither institution should have any influence in the other, as if the wall were impenetrable. It would be better to speak of "boundary lines" instead of "walls," and of mutual respect instead of "separation." Abraham Kuyper used the term "sphere sovereignty" to describe the mutual respect that institutions should have for each other.[23] The most important point is to protect the Church from the interference of the State in matters of ethics, faith and worship, but neither should the Church impose its religion on the people of a country.

This history also encourages us, as we see the progress in allowing greater freedom of religion in Europe and the Americas. Compare the situation in these countries with the reality in strict muslim countries like Saudi Arabia, Iran and Afghanistan, that repress alternative religious expression, and with totalitarian communist regimes, such as China, North Korea and Vietnam, that practice atheism and repress almost *all* religious expression. Let's be thankful, but let's remember the lessons learned!

---

[23] Abraham Kuyper, *Sphere Sovereignty* (Monergism Books, 2024).

4. WHEN IS WAR JUSTIFIED?

The fifth commandment (Exodus 20:13) says, "Thou shalt not kill" (KJV), or "You shall not murder" (ESV). Protecting life and seeking peace are fundamental moral principles. However, all the commandments should be understood in the context of the whole Bible, which will show that there are circumstances in which killing is permitted.

1) God Himself established punishment by death to be carried out by the corresponding authorities in Israel for someone who has committed crimes such as murder (Exodus 21:12).

2) It was legitimate for an individual to kill to defend himself, his family, and his home, at least in some circumstances.

Exodus 22:2
If a thief is caught breaking in and is struck so that he dies, the defender is not guilty of bloodshed. (NIV84)

3) God sometimes called the nation of Israel to engage in war in response to being attacked.

Numbers 31:1-2
The LORD spoke to Moses, saying, "Avenge the people of Israel on the Midianites. ..."

1 Samuel 15:2-3

This is what the L*ORD* *Almighty says: "I will punish the Amalekites for what they did to Israel when they waylaid them as they came up from Egypt. Now go, attack the Amalekites and totally destroy everything that belongs to them. ... (NIV84)*

4) The Israelites were commanded to defend and "rescue" the weak and needy.

Psalm 82:3-4

Give justice to the weak and the fatherless; maintain the right of the afflicted and the destitute. Rescue the weak and the needy; deliver them from the hand of the wicked.

Abraham took an army of 318 to rescue his nephew Lot from captivity (Genesis 14), and was blessed by Melchizedek.

Genesis 14:19-20

And he blessed him and said, "Blessed be Abram by God Most High, Possessor of heaven and earth; and blessed be God Most High, who has delivered your enemies into your hand!" ...

I conclude that *both personal and national self-defense are justified.* If someone breaks into my home and attempts to kill me or my family, I would be justified in killing him to avoid it, if necessary. The same applies to self-defense as a nation.

I also conclude that there are times when killing is justified to defend others. I would propose a guideline that *it is legitimate for a nation to engage in war when even more lives would be lost if they didn't.* In other words, the commandment "Thou shalt not kill" implies that we should also strive to keep others from killing. Sometimes it might be difficult to be sure how to apply this guideline, but other times it is obvious. For example, it was clearly legitimate to participate in a war to stop Hitler from continuing his military campaigns and the extermination of the Jews.

Some restrictions are given in the Mosaic law to avoid disproportionate punishments. That's really the purpose of the "lex talionis," to give a guideline for civil authorities. Punishment should be no more than "eye for eye, tooth for tooth" (Exodus 21:23-24, Leviticus 4:19-20). For example, if a man breaks a woman's arm, it wouldn't be fair to punish him by putting him to death. A similar principle should be applied in the case of international conflicts. If an enemy country has only destroyed a bridge, it wouldn't be fair to retaliate by killing a thousand people.

How about what Jesus said regarding "turning the other cheek" (Matthew 5:38-39)? He is not denying the right of *civil authorities* to punish criminals or the right of a *nation* to defend itself against foreign attacks, because these things were clearly permitted. Neither is He saying we shouldn't defend *others*. This is about how we should respond to a *personal offense* against ourselves.

Secondly, we shouldn't take this in an absolute and legalistic way. In the context, Jesus is giving *illustrations*, not specific detailed commandments. They had converted the guideline of "an eye for an eye" into an obligation instead of a limitation, and He is teaching us another *principle*, that we should seek peace without always insisting on our rights.

Thirdly, just as the commandments about lying and killing have exceptions, turning the other cheek also has exceptions. If somebody points a gun at me to kill me, I have a right to fight back.

Jesus scolded Peter for cutting off the servant's ear when they went to arrest Him (John 18:10-11), but He also told the disciples to take a sword with them on the road (Luke 22:36: "...Let the one who has no sword sell his cloak and buy one.") So it doesn't mean that we should just let people abuse us or never defend ourselves. For example, a woman who is being physically abused by her husband doesn't have to put up with it. Paul's exhortation applies here:

> Romans 12:18
> If possible, so far as it depends on you, live peaceably with all.

15. MODERN ISRAEL AND THEIR RIGHT TO LAND

Some evangelicals believe that the recent return of Jewish people to the land of Israel is a fulfillment of biblical prophecy, and that as Christians we should give our support to the nation of Israel in the conflicts taking place in that area. This view often goes along with the theological conviction that there is a separate future for Jewish Israel and for the Church. Some point out that the promise to Abraham was to give his descendants the land "forever" (Genesis 13:15). They also mention other prophecies about the Jews returning to Israel and having their fortunes restored (Ezekiel 36:24: "I will take you from the nations and gather you from all the countries and bring you into your own land," Jeremiah 29:14: ..."I will restore your fortunes and gather you from all the nations and all the places where I have driven you, declares the LORD, and I will bring you back to the place from which I sent you into exile.")

However, other theologians, with whom I agree, believe that the promises made to Abraham are fulfilled spiritually in all believers (Romans 2:28-29; 9:8, Galatians 3:9; 3:26-29; 6:16, Ephesians 2:11-16). They believe that prophecies such as Ezekiel 36:24 and Jeremiah 29:14 were already fulfilled when many returned from exile to rebuild the temple and the walls of Jerusalem centuries before Christ (Ezra, Nehemiah). They argue that, while Israel had a key role in the Old Testament development of the kingdom of God, the modern political nation of Israel today no longer represents the people of God and no longer has a divine right to the promises concerning the land of Old Testament Israel. When the Jewish people rejected Jesus as the Messiah, they broke the covenant and lost the right to their inheritance (Romans 9:30-33; 11:7). Their branch has been broken off, and the Gentiles have been grafted in from all ethnic groups and all nations (Romans 11:17-20).

There is one other prophecy that is more difficult to explain, one made by Jesus in Luke 21:24: "Jerusalem will be trampled underfoot by the Gentiles, until the times of the Gentiles are fulfilled." This is obviously a prophecy of something that was still in the future when Jesus spoke it. Some argue that the "times of the Gentiles" mentioned in this verse have already been fulfilled and that the Jews currently have God's blessing to take control of Jerusalem. They warn that we should not to try to interfere with the fulfillment of these prophecies.[24]

But is that what is happening now? No, the current events don't fit the prophecies. Romans 11:11-26 mentions what will happen when "the fullness of the Gentiles has come in." It indicates that after the full number of Gentiles are saved, there will be a great spiritual awakening among the Jews. They will be "grafted in" again ("all Israel will be saved"). But there has been no such revival among Jewish people yet. Furthermore, Luke 21:24 doesn't say that the Jews will take back the land of ancient Palestine, much less by means of war.

---

[24] See the video, "The Six Day War" <https://cbn.com/video/news/six-day-war>.

Having said this about Israel not having a divine right to the land of ancient Canaan in our times, I want to add that we should love the Jewish people and appreciate the place they have had in the plan of God to establish His kingdom and to give us our Savior. We should also have compassion on them for all the suffering they have experienced throughout history, especially under Hitler during World War II. We also know that there has always been a "remnant" of Jews who have believed in Christ (Romans 11:5), and we can rejoice in the promise that many more will eventually be saved (Romans 11:25-26).

16. OTHER PRACTICAL SUGGESTIONS

After becoming Christians, part of our spiritual growth includes a responsibility as citizens of our country. We can work toward improving our government without confusing politics with the kingdom of God. While we can't expect politics to transform people, we should definitely expect transformed people to make a positive impact on their government.

But how? Here are some suggestions:

a) One important way we can have a positive influence in our government is by informing ourselves and voting responsibly. I recommend examining the candidates' policies and their history. However, their character is just as important. It's their personal integrity that will determine how they make decisions and how they act as a politician. A candidate might make promises that we support, but if he is dishonest, he won't keep them. An evil person will inevitably exercise his or her office in an evil way.

b) There may also be occasions when it's appropriate to write to an elected official or participate in a *peaceful* protest.

c) Some Christians may even be called to hold public office, like Abraham Kuyper in Holland and many other Christians throughout the world.

d) We should "renew our minds" and teach biblical guidelines for ethical and social issues.

e) The Church also has a prophetic role in denouncing injustice, defending freedom, and promoting morality. However, when churches, pastors or leaders speak publicly or in representation of the People of God, they should be certain that they can defend what they say from Scripture, just like when they preach a sermon from the pulpit. *The Westminster Confession of Faith* recommends that church councils are not to "intermeddle" in civil affairs except in "extraordinary" cases.

> Synods and councils are to handle, or conclude nothing, but that which is ecclesiastical: and are not to intermeddle with civil affairs which concern the commonwealth, unless by way of humble petition in cases extraordinary; or, by way of advice, for satisfaction of conscience, if they be thereunto required by the civil magistrate.[25]

f) It's a mistake when churches and church leaders publicly identify themselves with particular candidates or political parties. After spending time in many countries, I can testify that this can cause the Church to lose its credibility and its prophetic voice. Furthermore, you can never be sure how that candidate will actually behave during his time in office. We should keep ourselves above the divisive politics of this world, free to denounce sin and injustice on the part of any politician or political party. This will mean that we can be trusted to give spiritual counsel to any politician. We are citizens of a better kingdom. As Carl Trueman says, "The gospel

---

[25] Chapter 31, section 4. in the current version used by the *Presbyterian Church in America*. < WCFScripureProofs2022.pdf (pcaac.org) >, (Oct. 18, 2023).

cannot and must not be identified with partisan political posturing."[26]

g) If we as Christians want to help make our government better, we should encourage our politicians to make laws and policies that are aligned with God's Word. However, these laws should deal with justice and order between people and institutions, not personal matters or private religious matters where nobody is harmed or treated unjustly. In the United States, for example, we could try to influence for improving laws regarding topics such as abortion, just economic guidelines, racism, the care of the sick, and war.

h) As Calvin proposed, the civil government should only supervise *outward* morality. (But he wasn't consistent with this.) This means that not every sin needs to have a civil law against it. For example, the government shouldn't punish someone for having sinful thoughts like envy or anger. These thoughts are sinful, but they shouldn't be punished by the government as a crime. However, murder definitely should be punished. The government shouldn't punish people for believing in another religion instead of Christianity. In general, we shouldn't let the government decide what we believe or how we worship. However, if a member of another religion kills a Christian because they believe their religion requires it, they should be punished.

i) It's important to respect freedom of religion, even for other religions. We should try to influence for more

---

[26] Carl R. Trueman, *Republocrat; Confessions of a Liberal Conservative* (Philipsburg, NJ: P&R Publishing, 2010), p. xxv.

Christian values and more Christian morality, but that doesn't mean we should impose our faith on others.

Os Guinness, in *The Case for Civility*, argues that it is more important now than ever that Christians insist on our freedom of expression and freedom of religion, *and that we also grant this same freedom to others.* He considers that this is one of the most important issues of our day, and he is concerned that some Christian groups in the United States are confused regarding this topic. In the first place, we should treat others as we would want them to treat us, and this includes allowing freedom of convictions and religious practice. In the second place, if we do not protect this freedom for all people, it might be the Christians who lose our rights next time.[27]

---

[27] Os Guinness, *The Case for Civility* (New York: HarperOne, 2008.)

www.ingramcontent.com/pod-product-compliance
Lightning Source LLC
Chambersburg PA
CBHW061335140726
47997CB00003B/996